Hare Publishing.

To Louis

May you grow with Loveall light in your heart.

AUTHORS NOTE

WE ALL START LIFE WITH THE ABILITY TO GROW PHYSICALLY, EMOTIONALLY AND WITH SOCIAL CONNECTIONS COMMUNICATING WITH OUR PHYSICAL AND SOCIAL OTHERS AND WORLD.

POOR MENTAL HEALTH COMES FROM SPIKE.. WE AS HUMAN BEINGS HOLD ONTO THE EMOTIONAL REACTIONS AND DO NOT LET GO. WHEN WE HOLD ON TO LIFE'S SPIKES, WE PASS ON, WE BLAME AND SHAME, WE GET BITTER, WE CAN BE REVENGEFUL, WE NEGATIVELY PAYBACK, WE CAN THINK PEOPLE AND SOCIETY OWES US. SPIKE GROWS AND LOVEALL DIMS.

POSITIVE MENTAL HEALTH COMES FROM LOVEALL. LIVING IN THE HERE AND NOW, LETTING GO OF THE EMOTIONS FROM THE PAST; NOT CONTINUING WITH HOLDING ON OF THE EMOTIONAL REACTIONS AND BEHAVIOURS OF OTHERS OR OURSELVES. WHEN WE USE LOVEALL WE CAN RELEASE OURSELVES FROM SPIKES HOLD. THIS BRINGING AN INNER PEACE AND CALMNESS, ALLOWING SPACE TO POSITIVELY GIVE AND RECEIVE. LOVEALL SHINES BRIGHTLY AND SPIKES DO NOT GROW.

WHEN WE HOLD ON SO TIGHTLY TO THE PAST WE CAN NOT MOVE ON. IT TAKES AWAY THE POSITIVITY OF THE HERE AND NOW AND NEGATIVELY IMPACTS THE FUTURE..
WHEN WE LET GO OF THE PAST, WE HAVE THE FREEDOM IN THE HERE AND NOW AND CHOICE OF A POSITIVE FUTURE.

LOVEALL AND SPIKE TEACHES CHILDREN TO RESPECT OTHERS AS WELL AS THEMSELVES. IT TEACHES THEM NOT ONLY THAT THEIR EMOTIONAL REACTIONS AND BEHAVIOURS IMPACT OTHER HUMANS, BUT ALSO IMPACTS THEMSELVES.

WHEN THEY ARE NEGATIVE OUTWARDLY THEY ALSO CAUSE AN INTERNAL NEGATIVITY. HOWEVER WHEN THEY ARE POSITIVE OUTWARDLY THEY ALSO CAUSE AN INTERNAL POSITIVITY.

LOVEALL AND SPIKE START TO SHOW CHILDREN THAT THOUGH YOU CAN GROW SPIKES; YOU CAN ALSO REDUCE SPIKES.. WHEN THINGS GO WRONG YOU CAN CHOOSE TO CHANGE IT. IT DOES NOT HAVE TO STAY WITH YOU. YOU CAN LET IT GO. YOU CAN DO SOMETHING POSITIVE AND STOP THE PASSING OF THE SPIKE.

INSPIRATION QUOTES

AN OLD MAN TOLD HIS GRANDSON

"MY SON THERE IS A BATTLE BETWEEN TWO WOLVES INSIDE OF US ALL"

"ONE IS FULL OF EVIL. JEALOUSY, ANGRY, GREEDY, REVENGEFUL, INFERIORITY, LIES AND

EGO"

"THE OTHER IS FULL OF GOODNESS.

JOY, PEACE, COMPASSION, LOVE, HOPE AND TRUTH"

THE BOY THOUGHT ABOUT IT FOR A LONG TIME.

THEN ASKED HIS GRANDFATHER "WHICH WOLF WINS?"

THE OLD MAN REPLIED QUIETLY

"THE ONE YOU FEED SON, THE ONE YOU FEED"

ANON.

Spike & Loveall

Written and Illustrated

By

Nettie Forsyth

Did you know circle is a 2 Dimensional shape?

It has curved lines that never stop.

It keeps going around and around.

Look! Here are some circles.

Did you know that a 3D circle is a sphere?

It too keeps going around and around.

Here are some spheres.

Did you know there are two very special spheres?

No?

Let me introduce these invisible spheres to you;

This is Spike and Loveall.

Now, we all carry around these two invisible spheres;

you do,

I do,

everyone does.

They follow us everywhere we go.

Spike and Loveall look and act very differently!

Each person's Spike and Loveall spheres look differently inside and can vary in size.

Let's look at Spike.

On the outside Spike looks very interesting.

Spike has Spikes!

When Spike gets used, Spike makes more spikes.

When Spike does not get used Spike does not grow more spikes.

Now lets look at Loveall.

On the outside Loveall looks very interesting .

Loveall is made up of lots of light.

When Loveall gets used, Loveall makes more light.

When Loveall does not get used,

Loveall gets dull and is not very bright.

HELPING

SHOPPING

LEARNING

FRIENDSHIP

Now the trouble is that when Spike gets too big

Spike starts bumping into other people's Spikes.

In return it makes mine and yours Spike grow.

When other people's Spike bumps into yours; it will make your

Spike even bigger if you are not careful!

Lets take a look inside a Spike. What makes Spike grow?

The other trouble with your Spike and other people's Spike; it likes to take Loveall's light.

So you have to look after Loveall very carefully.

When other people's Spike tries to give you some of their Spike and tries to take your Loveall, you can say "no thanks".

To not make your Spike grow you have to use your Loveall.

You can choose to leave and walk away.

You can choose not to copy.

You can chose not to take revenge, not hold grudges or retaliate.

You can really use your Loveall.

You can choose forgiveness

and you can choose to be friendly in return instead.

Loveall can never be too big.

Loveall's bumping is gentle and kind. Loveall passes light on to other people's Lovealls.

As well as making your Loveall grow even bigger!

You have to use your Loveall all of the time to make it shine brightly.

Let's take a look inside a Loveall. What makes Loveall grow?

Now the great thing is you can use the light of your Loveall when other people use their Spike.

You can be friendly back, you can talk to someone and get help for the Spike, you can tell their Spike you forgive them for Spiking.

If you have used your Spike you can use your Loveall to own up, say you are sorry and try to make it better.

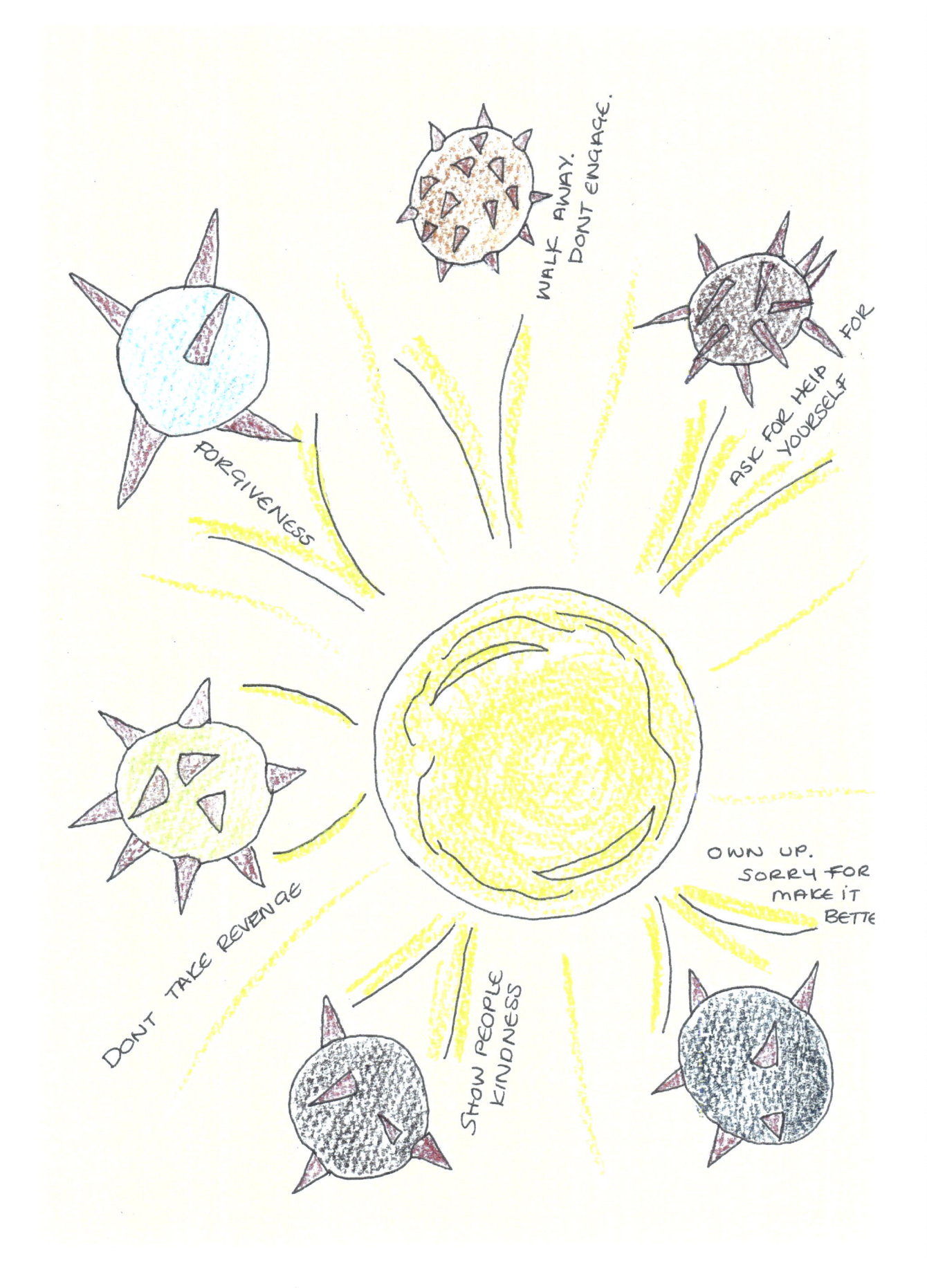

Now you see how Spike and Loveall work!

So we need to use less Spike and more Loveall.

Exercise:

1. Can you draw a picture of your Spike and your Loveall? What would they look like?

2. Can you think of anything that goes inside of your Spike? You might like to write it in a spike or draw a picture in your Spike.

3. Can you think of anything that goes inside of your Loveall? You might like to write it down or draw a picture.

4. Can you think of anything that can make your Spike smaller?

5. Can you think of anything that can make your Loveall Bigger?

ACKNOWLEDGEMENT'S

TO ALL THE CHILDREN I HAVE BEEN PRIVILEGED TO WORK WITH
IN THE 30 YEARS OF MY CAREER.

THANK YOU FOR BEING THE INSPIRATIONS OF MY STORIES.

ABOUT THE AUTHOR

Nettie Forsyth is a passionate advocate of Families, Children and Child development.

Known for her simplistic but vast knowledge base of Children, Child Development, Behaviour and Emotion work.

Nettie is appreciated by many she has worked with in her therapeutic behaviour strategy and now Counselling work.

Those who have had the privilege come away as very different people enabled and empowered.

The families functions and changes have been amazing within her work, whether it be child, siblings or parents.

Her Behaviour blog and common sense to parenting has empowered many parents.

As a parent herself got thrown into Adoption issues, SEN and Aspergers which bought its own learning. This was used as a learning tool and gave Nettie more insight in to the world of Challenging Behaviour.
Her own Daughter becoming a successful young adult.

This all inspires the books she writes.

Contacts:

Challenging-Behaviour@hotmail.co.uk

www.help-with-challenging-behaviour.co.uk